Keetley, Utah

A LETTER
TO OPHELIA

ISBN-13: 978-0-9975278-1-0
ISBN-10: 0-9975278-1-0

Published by TheHappyProject.com

Printed in the United States of America

A LETTER TO OPHELIA

from Keetley, Utah

Preface

The following article is a chronicle of events, together with my personal comments, depicting the actual story of the progress made in the first year of existence of Keetley Farms at Keetley, Wasatch County, Utah, by a group of voluntary Japanese evacuees in the spring of 1942. All facts are true, and the opinions and the comments expressed are those of the author and the people he had interviewed.

It is written in a letter form to my mythical friend, Miss Ophelia ____________, supposedly a resident of Heart Mountain Relocation Center, Wyoming.

All the anecdotes written herein are actual happenings at Keetley, but the characters mentioned...if there is any similarity to any person or persons dead or living in Keetley... **MAY** be purely coincidental.

This article has been written so that my many friends, especially those in the Relocation Centers, may be informed of what we are, and what we have been doing out here in Keetley Valley. Since I wish to keep these papers as a memento of Keetley, Utah, I only ask that everyone who reads this article...my friends and friends of my friends...kindly to sign his or her name on the last few pages reserved for this purpose. The pictures shown at the end of this article were all snapped in the early part of January of this year.

Masao Tsujimoto
Keetley Farms
Keetley, Utah
1943

Artist's conception of
Keetley in Winter (Snowbound).
Note: Scenery obliterated by snow.

March 31, 1943

Dear Ophelia:

I'm sorry I couldn't write to you for such a long time. Since I didn't know your address either at Pomona Assembly Center or at Heart Mountain Relocation Center . . . (I knew that you were somewhere in Pomona Assembly Center) until Archibald wrote to me about you and forwarded me your present address at Heart Mountain, Wyoming.

Gosh, the last time I saw you was sometime in February of last year in San Francisco, wasn't it? Do you remember that at that time I mentioned to you a possible voluntary evacuation to Utah? Well, the plan did come through. Since I have plenty of time on my hands now, I might as well tell you all about it.

It was during the latter days of March of last year that we suddenly set the date for our departure for Keetley, Wasatch County, Utah. We left Oakland on Saturday afternoon, March 28, taking the route via Sacramento. There were twenty-one people in our group, and we traveled in two sedans and three trucks. The latter were loaded with our personal belongings and furniture. I drove one of the sedans.

That night we stayed at a motel in Truckee, California. It was a very nice, comfortable place, and incidentally very expensive. And we all slept well. We spent Sunday night at a motor court in Winnemucca, Nevada. I still remember that we had dinner at a Chop Suey place in that town and they charged us fifteen cents for a small dish (not a bowl, mind you) of rice, and each of us ate two to three (and even four) dishes of rice too.

The following evening we arrived at Salt Lake City, and since we didn't know the road to Keetley, especially at night, we spent that evening at a motor court inside the city. We came to Keetley on Tuesday afternoon, the last day of March, exactly one year ago today. We had a slow but very leisurely eight hundred mile trip which required three full days. This had been my first out-of-state trip, and for the first time in my life I realized what beautiful scenery we have back in good ole California. Nevada and Utah were practically all sage brushed deserts. We hardly saw an evergreen tree in the eastern part of Nevada or in the western part of Utah--nothing but mile after mile of sagebrush and jackrabbits.

Contrary to rumors we used to hear in San Francisco before our evacuation about anti-Japanese sentiments and activities both in Nevada and Utah, we encountered no such cases. We heard that service stations refused to sell gasoline and auto courts barred their doors to Japanese, but we received excellent service and treatment all along our trip to Keetley.

I remember that we filled up all our gas tanks just before we hit Nevada--just a precautionary measure, which we found out later was quite unnecessary.

At Keetley, that same afternoon, we were joined by the rest of our party of a little over a hundred people. We had traveled in about five or six separate caravans totaling eighteen passenger cars, eleven trucks, and two house trailers. It was very cold then; the grounds were still covered with snow. The water systems of the up-till now unoccupied houses were all frozen, and a few of the cabins were really "snowbound." The pick and shovel crew had to get busy making roads to them. We occupied a large, two-story apartment building consisting of ten apartments of three rooms each. There was also three large bungalows and five small cabins.

We were very busy the first few weeks. We couldn't start the farm work, but we had plenty of other things to do. We had to go up to the railway depot of Keetley, one and a half miles from our settlement, to unload the freight cars. Since there were two grocers in our party, they brought along two carloads of groceries which were, for the most part, Japanese canned goods: shoyu, rice, noodles, etc. I suppose we unloaded more than half a dozen freight cars loaded with groceries, farm implements, furniture, and other personal belongings. As far as I was concerned, unloading the freight wasn't so bad. Since most of us met each other for the first time, we weren't acquainted with each other. Due to my puny size, the rest of the fellows thought that I was a fifteen-year old punk and wouldn't let me handle any heavy boxes and things. Whenever I carried a sack of rice, somebody always came to my rescue. And I'm supposed to be an ex-expressman too! The young kid who used to follow me around didn't fare so well. Although he was thirteen years old, he was much larger than I, and did he get the works! Poor kid! That was one time I realized the advantage of being small.

One of the boys slipped on the ice while carrying a very heavy box of bottled shoyu on his shoulders and broke his ankle bone. The very first thing that came to his mind, after he took the spill, was whether the bottles were broken or not. He didn't even think about his broken leg! He was laid up for quite awhile.

We built two additional cabins and an eleven-car garage behind the apartment building. The rest of the cars, trucks, and tractors were housed in the barns and sheds. We also fixed the basement of the apartment preparatory for storage of our groceries and excess personal belongings. Although the apartment was already equipped with cold and hot showers, we built a large Japanese bath for the convenience of all.

Whose idea was it to come out here to Utah and start this farming project? Who was the leader of our group? Perhaps I should write something about my eldest brother's brother-in-law, Fred Isamu Wada of Oakland, who originated and succeeded in establishing this enterprise which was soon to be called the one and only "Keetley Farms". Today her name and fame has spread far and near throughout our nation, from the coasts of Oregon to the sunny beaches of Florida and from the shores of California to the metropolis of New York. This project was the first and the only successful one to be undertaken by an individual. Perhaps a few of the excerpts from Dr. Galen M. Fisher's recent article, "The Japanese That More People Want," can more appropriately describe what Fred Wada has done in preparation for the organization of this settlement.

Two months after Pearl Harbor, President Roosevelt gave the Army the power to remove any persons of Japanese descent from the West Coast. This drastic measure was due to various causes, chief among which was fear of a Japanese invasion aided by fifth columnists and sinister anti-hysteria threatening violence against Japanese residents on the coast.

The deadline set by the Army of "voluntary evacuation" was the 29th of March. After that date, all Japanese had to go to guarded Assembly Centers and later to permanent Relocation Centers. Fred Wada, citizen and prosperous produce merchant of Oakland, decided to move out of California before the deadline, and to help a company of other Japanese do likewise.

Born in Bellingham, Washington, thirty-five years ago, of Roman Catholic parents, Fred was left motherless while still a young child. At fourteen he quit school and went to work. By the time he was twenty-seven, he had forged to the front and became president of the East Bay Food Dealers Association in Oakland.

The war broke out. Fred's younger brother Bill volunteered in March 1941, and another brother Ben was drafted in January 1942. Ben is now a corporal at Camp Grant, Illinois. Fred himself would have liked to enlist, but he had a wife and three children, and he also knew that he might not be welcomed in the Army, so he quickly reasoned: "The President says that the output of both munitions and food must be stepped up. I can't make munitions, but I can raise food: I'll make it my patriotic duty and goal to find unused land, form a corps of Japanese like myself, and try to break all records at raising crops, without costing Uncle Sam a red cent. We won't wait to be rounded up by the Army and become expensive wards of the Government. We'll go eastward of our own free will and break land like the early pioneers. Our motto will be, 'Go east, young man, and raise food for freedom." That was about March 10.

Action followed at once. Fred saw in a newspaper that the farmers of Duchesne County, Utah wanted farm labor very badly. He took a train for Salt Lake City. Expecting to receive a ready welcome from the descendants of the persecuted Mormon refugees led by Brigham Young, he at first met only rebuffs. To begin with, some of the Japanese residents threw cold water on the plan, saying, "We are getting along pretty well, but if many more Japanese come into the state, public hostilities will be aroused and all of us will suffer."

The Ogden Chapter of the J.A.C.L. also resented our coming into their state. When the Secretary of the Utah Defense Council, Laurence A. Johnson, heard Fred's story, he remarked noncommittally, "Most of the Japanese who come here from California are concerned only about getting jobs for themselves. You seem to be planning to make jobs for other people. You're certainly a rare bird. Perhaps you can make a go of it. I advise you to confer with David Trevithick, Director of the State Department of Social Welfare."

In accordance with the suggestion of Mr. Johnson, Fred went up to the State Capitol and discussed his plans with Mr. Trevithick. He called in some of his associates, and they were so interested that although it was Saturday, they forgot their lunch and let all the clerks go home before they finally adjourned the meeting at 2:30 in the afternoon. Mr. Trevithick said he would back Fred 100%, and he sat down and wrote Fred a letter of introduction to the Commissioner of Duchesne County, in which he commended Fred's plans.

With rising hopes, Fred rented an automobile and motored from Salt Lake City along U.S. Highway 40 toward Duchesne County through snowdrifts ten feet high, for it was early in March. Thirty-nine miles out, he stopped at Keetley to see George A. Fisher. He was formerly the Executive Secretary of the Utah State Land Board but is now a rancher and the proud owner and Mayor of the microscopic village of Keetley, located southeast of Salt Lake City. Mr. Fisher naturally wanted to get someone to lease and till his big ranch, but he was also genuinely interested in giving the ousted Japanese Americans a chance to make a fresh start. He urged Fred to settle on his ranch instead of going further; but while Fred appreciated this offer, he said that he had promised to discuss matters at a meeting of the citizens of the Duchesne and her neighboring Uintah County and so must go on, but would see him on his way back.

At Duchesne's County Seat, the town of Roosevelt, one hundred and fifty miles east of Keetley, he found three hundred and fifty folks gathered to hear him. He said something like this, "As you will see, I am not much of a speaker, for I was left an orphan and could not finish my schooling, but I am a good American citizen, and I simply want to tell you that my foremost desire in this crisis of our national life is to help win the war by raising more food. For that purpose, I want to bring a company of other good Americans of Japanese stock from California to settle and farm in your state. All but a few of them are citizens of the United States and good Christians. They are hard-working and law-abiding, and will cooperate in community affairs. They will bring an average of $1,500 in cash or equipment and will never go on the relief rolls."

One listener rose and asked, "What about the Japanese fifth columnists at Pearl Harbor?" Fred replied that he believed those charges had been cooked up by the politicians and yellow journalists, and that certainly none of his group would do anything to harm the country. Unfortunately, at that time, those false reports about sabotage by Japanese at Pearl Harbor had not been denied, as they were a little later by Secretaries Knox and Stimson and the Honolulu Chief of Police. A county surveyor from Ogden, who happened to be present at the meeting, then said, "I lost two sons at Pearl Harbor, and every time I see a man of the Japanese race, I shiver, but after hearing your story, I'm ready to let a good many

Japs from California come in here. We need them." Still another listener exclaimed, "I'm a Legionnaire, and until I heard Mr. Wada I was dead against any Japs coming in, but now I'm in favor of it." Fred asked him if he were willing to wire that to Governor Maw of Utah, and he said that he would. A journalist in the audience was so favorably impressed that he at once reported his feeling to Governor Maw by a long-distance telephone call. After the meeting, forty farmers stayed and pressed Fred to lease or buy their farms, which ranged from one hundred to two thousand acres.

The good people of Duchesne County were so fair-minded and friendly that Fred was tempted to settle there. One great drawback was that the nearest railroad to ship our produce was more than one hundred and twenty miles away and the distance to Salt Lake City was too great. We would also have to erect most of our own dwellings. So Fred decided to go back and talk again with George A. Fisher. George put his case like this, "Almost all of my thirty-eight hundred acres are good, black loam, and about half can be irrigated at low cost. The bottom lands will be excellent for truck gardening, and the hill slopes for hay and livestock grazing. Then these fifteen cottages and a ten-suite apartment will go with the lease. I built them years ago to house the miners of yonder mines, but they curtailed operations during the tourist season. The lease is yours for $2 an acre, and I will throw in the buildings and my own personal services in making your path smooth as long as you stay here. But first of all, I suppose I ought to check up a bit on you and the people you are proposing to bring with you." Mr. Fisher's offer appealed to Fred so much that he paid him $500 on the spot to clinch the deal, but they agreed to consider the lease tentative until after George A. could go to California with Fred to make his own assessment as to how the Japanese had gotten along with the white folks there.

Then Mr. Trevithick, Mr. Fisher, and Fred went to present the plans to Governor Maw, who listened carefully but expressed fears that some of the people Fred was intending to bring there would be disloyal. Fred replied that if any of them should make any trouble or prove to be disloyal, he'd be glad to face the firing squad. Finally, the Governor said that he could not allow any Japanese to settle near the vital defense industrial areas in Northern Utah but they could go anywhere else, provided that he could clear the matter with all the County Commissioners and if the local inhabitants raised no serous objections. This decision was fair, and it gave Fred immense relief. On March 16th, the Governor held a conference with the Commissioners from the twenty-nine counties and found that of them all, only Duchesne and Uintah counties were ready to welcome the Japanese settlers. This unfavorable verdict did not discourage Fred. He felt certain that if the colony he was planning to form were given a chance in Duchesne or in any other county, it would soon convince the skeptics and a lot of them would be clamoring to have Japanese come and meet the farm labor shortage existing in their counties. Fred was right, for last summer we were simply swamped with requests for labor by the farmers of other counties.

Fred went back to California, and soon after George A. Fisher arrived there. Fred took him around several counties so that he could ask a lot of white folks what they thought of the Japanese they knew. District Attorney John Lewis of San Benito County told him, "For seven years I have been the District Attorney, and I have never had any occasion to prosecute a single Japanese, nor have I heard of an arrest in this district of a Japanese on any charge." The Oakland Community Chest Executive told him that the Japanese never went on relief. At the end of his inquires, Mr. Fisher wired Governor Maw that he was fully satisfied. Fred then executed a lease for one year with an option for four more years.

At that point, Fred was puzzled over the best way to organize the colony, so he asked for the counsel of Dr. Galen M. Fisher of Oakland. Dr. Fisher was a humanitarian, president of the Pacific School of Religion in Berkley, vice-president of the Protestant Wartime Commission, a writer, executive secretary of the Northern California Committee for Fair

Play, and the executive secretary of the Institute of Pacific Relations. Fred explained to him that he was not thinking of profits at all; in fact, he was ready to sink $2,000 in this project. Dr. Fisher's advice was that Fred make it a non-profit enterprise which Fred decided to do.

Then the personnel of our colony was chosen. Enrolled were one hundred and thirty associates--forty-five able-bodied men, of whom twenty-five were single, thirty married women, twenty single women, and thirty-five children. About twenty-five of the men were farmers. There were students and graduates of agricultural schools, merchants, fishermen, fish dealers, express-men, a plumber, electrician, barber, pharmacist, auto mechanic, carpenter, and gardener. They all agreed to pool their machines and stocks of food and to contribute so much per capita for general expenses. It was to be "all for one and one for all." Incidentally, Fred's trip to Utah for making arrangements was made at his own personal expense.

Time was slipping fast toward the deadline of March 29, after which General DeWitt had forbidden any further voluntary movement of Japanese from the Coast. Therefore, beginning with the party of twenty-one people (our group), our entire company reached Keetley on March 31. Only one member of the colony failed to get out of California before the freezing date and a failure to do so was all to his credit. It was this way. He owned a valuable seeding machine, so complicated that only he could run it. The neighboring white farmers begged him to stay until he could finish seeding their fields. Loyalty to his neighbors and eagerness to help increase the nation's food supply made him decide to stay behind, even though he knew he would have to go to the Assembly Center, behind barbed wires, instead of going as a free man with the rest of us. It was only after urgent appeals by Fred Wada that he was finally released and allowed to join his family here at Keetley a month later. He brought along with him $4,000 worth of farm machiney.

BEER

Well, Ophelia, I suppose I told you enough about what Fred has done for us. Now I'll tell you more about what we are doing and what we have accomplished in the past year. But first let me describe Keetley and it's surroundings to you.

As I said before, Keetley is situated thirty-nine miles southeast of Salt Lake City, right by U.S. Highway 40. Traffic is relatively heavy on this highway since this is the main road to Denver, five hundred miles away. Due to this reason, we have had the pleasure of a few unexpected visits by some of our friends who were en route to Denver and happened to drop in at our settlement--purely by accident. Were they surprised to find us here! Our colony is located by the junction of U.S. Highway 40 and the unpaved country road leading to the village of Keetley one and a half miles away. Right across the apartment building, there is a combination gas service station and grocery store operated by Mr. and Mrs. John R. O'Toole. Since they carry practically all our everyday needs as far as food is concerned (milk, bread, etc.), they save us the inconvenience of shopping trips to nearby Heber City, twelve miles away, or to Park City, ten miles in the opposite direction. Behind the grocery store is an old school building which is presently used as a garage for the county school bus. This school was in operation many years ago when there were more people here but has been closed since the depression of 1929. Heber City is newer and cleaner than Park City, and the road there from Keetley is better. Hence, we do most of our shopping there. The merchants there are all very nice and considerate to us.

Heber City is a very typical small American community--just like the ones you see in the movies. The population here is about two thousand and everybody knows everyone else. Only the main road is paved in this town, the others being dirt roads without even a sidewalk. The residential area is very serene and peaceful; you may see a cow or two browsing around in quest of grass. Cows, pigs, sheep and chickens are kept by the townspeople in their back and even in their front yards. Everyone here has a Victory garden. Practically all the townspeople are of the Mormon religion.

It may be surprising for you to know that the Mormon Church owns quite a few of the largest stores (including department stores) all over the State of Utah. The largest general store (and a very modern one, too) in Heber City is owned by the Mormon group. Evidence that the Mormons control the town is shown by the fact that no public athletic contests or events are held in Heber City on Sundays. Heber City can boast of a few nationally known stores such as the Safeway store and the J. C. Penny department store. It also has two modern drugstores.

There are also two dentists and three physicians practicing here. A hospital completes the medical facilities. All our medical cases are sent to one of the doctors here, and he sure is kept busy. We were all inoculated by him for typhoid fever and smallpox as a precautionary measure soon after we came here. He was ably assisted by yours truly. Among many of the cases he treated were a broken leg, broken arm, blood poisoning, maternity cases, cuts on the head, appendectomy, eczema, measles, asthma, common colds, stomach disorders, and minor treatments too numerous to mention.

Practically all the town residents and neighboring farmers dress alike here. With the exception of professional men, all the menfolks wear blue overalls and blue or gray working shirts. You seldom see a man on the street wearing a suit. If you do, they are as rare as hairs on Mussolini's pate. Heber isn't exactly old-fashioned, but most of the people do their traveling on bicycles. The manager of the Safeway store comes to work pedaling a bicycle. Even lady school teachers come to school on such gasless foot-propelled vehicles. This was before the gas rationing went into effect too. I had the opportunity to see a movie at Heber City once. At least one thing will always remain in my mind: the cowpunchers and farmers around here don't bother to change their clothes when they go to the movies. Hence, the odor of something reminding you of the stables is very distinct.

Coming back to Keetley . . . we are hemmed in on all four sides by high mountains. We are at a relatively high altitude, about 6,500 feet, which caused an uncountable number of illnesses among us at first. The nearby mountains where the mines are situated are more than 8,000 feet high. The metals mined there are mostly lead, silver, copper, and zinc. A peculiar fact about these mines is that the shafts are dug horizontally at the base instead of vertically from the top of the mountain. The nearby town of Park City is well known for her silver mines. The white population of Keetley was about a hundred; since our arrival, we have more than doubled the population. Near the mines there are a few dozen houses occupied by miners. The buildings in our community (some occupied by whites) are all built within an area of two square blocks, so you can readily see that some of our Japanese neighbors may live about two blocks away.

Since Fisher Ranch was a summer tourist camp as well as a cattle ranch, fish and game are plentiful here. A fair-sized creek, abundant with trout, runs near our houses. We planted more than twenty thousand trout in this creek last summer in preparation for this year's fishing sport. Last spring, most of the boys bought angling licenses. Fish dinners were common in Keetley for awhile. To tell you the truth, Ophelia, I must admit that I didn't catch a single trout with a hook, line, and sinker--although several attempts were made. But, I trapped almost a dozen big trout with dirt and shovel, of course during working hours.

A number of saddle horses are kept on this ranch. One of them is owned by Fred Wada and the rest by Mr. Fisher. All of us had ample opportunities to go horseback riding which seems to be enjoyable only for short jaunts. It was a common sight to see some of us fall off and bow at the horse's feet as if we were praying and thanking the beast for rides. We are getting used to seeing a riderless horse come trotting home followed by the cussing ex-rider an hour or so later. The foremost rider among us is a ten year old "little Tom Mix," a former Oaklander. There are so many bow-legged riding enthusiasts that now they actually make fun of the ones with straight legs.

Mr. Fisher also owns a very rare animal, a spotted jackass, and I don't mean the freckle-faced hakujin neighbor kid, either. However, the animal passed away early this year of old age. I am mentioning this since I thought that all relatives of the deceased should be immediately notified.

Prairie dogs are very common here. I remember that one day as I was coming home with another kid, we were able to count one hundred and fifty one prairie dogs running across the road before we walked the distance equivalent to two city blocks. These prairie dogs are very similar to squirrels except they lack the bushy tails. Last spring they raised havoc with our pea and lettuce crops. We used poison grain against them and killed quite a number of them, but it seemed that there were simply more prairie dogs than we had poison grain. The State Department of Agriculture supplied us with the poison, but since they were rationed to all the farms, we couldn't get as much as we needed.

Deer are very abundant here too. They destroyed a good deal of our lettuce crop. When hunting season opened last year, our white neighbors were kind enough to share their venison with our group. Our family enjoyed about five venison steak dinners which were indeed delicious. Some of us were fortunate enough to have pheasant which they received from the neighbors for dinner. It's too bad that the nisei aren't allowed to possess firearms, since Fisher Ranch is truthfully a hunter's paradise. It is not uncommon to hear the coyotes howling at night since they prey on sheep grazing on our ranch.

I suppose I gave you the general picture that the State of Utah is filled with nothing but sagebrush. If I did, please accept my humblest apology for en route to Provo from Keetley, we really do find some of the most beautiful scenery east of the High Sierras and west of the Rockies. I am referring to the Provo Canyon, which can justly be called, and is called, "The Yosemite of Utah." There are lots of high, magnificent waterfalls there, one of them being called, "The Bridal Veil Falls". All of these waterfalls drop into the Provo River which runs though the canyon. Ideal fishing spots and camping grounds may be found all along the river banks shaded by towering evergreen trees, and during the angling season, they are crowded with vacationers.

In the background may be seen the lofty majestic Mt. Timpanogos, the highest mountain in this state, which is more than 12,000 feet in altitude. On a clear day, this mountain can be faintly outlined from the town of Delta, more than a hundred miles away.

Since I know that you will be interested in Salt Lake City, the capital of Utah, I might as well tell you something about this city. Compared to California cities, it is pretty small. But it is, nevertheless, the largest city in the Sate of Utah. The other major towns in order of their population are Ogden, Provo, Logan, Camp Keams (an Army training center), and then Topaz Relocation Center.

Salt Lake City has several modern theatres, but compared with the West Coast movie houses, they are all relatively small in size. However, the films are shown here before they are distributed in California. We have seen quite a number of shows since we came here. Due to heavy traffic and the parking meters which charge at the rate of a penny for every twelve minutes in the downtown district, we usually park our cars in Japanese town, two blocks away, every time we go to the downtown area. Nihonmachi is very dirty and dingy, typical of most Japanese communities in California. The buildings are very old. The Japanese population was increased four or five fold, due to the influx of evacuees both voluntary and on furlough from relocation centers. Many of them are employed in restaurants, hotels, cleaning establishments, laundries, and garages. Many nisei girls are also working as domestics. There are many nisei, mostly from camps, who are just loafing and bumming around on the streets of Salt Lake City, and they do make a bad impression of the Japanese populace, as a whole, in the eyes of the American residents here. This may be the reason why it is getting more and more difficult for camp people to receive furlough permits.

There are many chop suey and noodle places operated by Japanese, but the oriental food served there is terrible. The prices are also pretty exorbitant. The variety in their Chinese dishes is very, very limited. Only Japanese rice is served. Chow mein is not as tasty compared to what we used to get in California. If you order "tofuyo", you have to dig around for the tofu. If you're lucky you may find some.

As a matter of fact, Japanese, not Chinese, tofu is used. There is a mochiya and a Japanese confectionery store, a tofu-ya, a Japanese tri-weekly newspaper (The Utah Nippo), a small fish market, barber shops, and numerous Japanese operated groceries, hotels, restaurants, cleaners, and laundries. The fish market seems to be doing the most flourishing business in Japanese town. The fish isn't especially fresh but miraculously sells very well. There are many truck-farmers in the outskirts and within Salt Lake City.

What was the reaction of the white people toward us? This may be of interest to you. Before our arrival, all the white people were against our coming here, except George A. Fisher, his family, and one other white family. The head of this family was a naval reserve officer, and he had numerous opportunities to contact Japanese when he was stationed at Honolulu, Mare Island, San Diego, and other points on the West Coast. The rest of the people here had never seen a person of Japanese ancestry before and naturally didn't understand us. I suppose they thought that we all had ideas and motives like Tojo. In fact, one neighbor lady told me one day that the first time she had seen a Japanese was sometime before our arrival when a couple of Japanese, one of them bearing scars on his face, stopped over at her store for a cup of coffee. They had hideous, suspicious looks, and their manners, she said, were far from pleasing. So she thought naturally that all Japanese were like them. She found out how wrong she had been when she became acquainted with us, she admitted . . . (ahem) . . .

You probably heard about the dynamite incidents here at Keetley. Because there are lots of mines here, sticks of dynamite are easily accessible. Two days before we came here, a charge of dynamite was blown off near our present dwellings. A few nights after our arrival, another blast went off on the highway about a quarter of a mile from here. We sure heard that blast. I suppose they were meant to intimidate us, but we weren't scared . . . too much.

A highway patrolman was then stationed here for a few days, but nothing happened. As time went on, we became more and more friendly with our neighbors. We leveled the ground and have built a two basket basketball court.

Almost every day after work, we played either baseball or basketball with the American Keetley boys. On one of their boy's birthday, all of us were invited by his dad to a wiener bake. They furnished all the entertainment such as music and songs, both solos and school pep songs, etc. One of the girls even gave us an exhibition in tap dancing, and we all enjoyed the evening very much. We presented the kid with a baseball and a bat as a birthday gift. One day, one of the boy's mother asked her son if it was fun to play with "those Jap boys," and the kid came right back with his comment, "They're not Jap boys . . . we're all Americans."

Three weeks after our arrival, the snow slowly started to melt, so we began our farming work. There were lots of things that we had to do. Suitable flat pasture lands were burned, rocks removed, and the soil leveled and plowed. Acre after acre of sagebrush-covered ground had to be prepared for plowing. Five tractors toiled day after day from sunrise to sunset uprooting the sagebrush which was then pulled up by hand, heaped into large piles and then burned. Rocks, large and small, had to be removed. In certain patches, truckload after truckload of alfalfa roots had to be carted out from the fields and dumped outside on the road. In one of the forty acre patches, more than fifty tons of rocks were taken out. After plowing, seeds of all kinds of vegetables were planted: peas, spinach, turnips, red beets, lettuce, cabbage, carrots, potatoes, red-tipped radishes, corn, daikon, onion, and barley. Young strawberry plants were also transplanted. The womenfolk were busy in their spare time knitting socks and sweaters for the American Red Cross. They knitted under the supervision of the wife of a very prominent Heber City physician.

Since we had more than one thousand acres of hay crop, the irrigation ditches for them had to be cleaned and dug. Incidentally, our drinking water flows through the sagebrushed pasture, and sometimes after the cattle have had a field day near its vicinity, strange unpleasant things come out of our water faucets. No wonder many of us had diarrhea at one time or another.

By the way, there are certain aspects of farming here in Utah that are quite different from the methods used in California. Back home, I guess you never heard of irrigating a hay ranch. Well, they do so out here. In California, all the fruit orchards are plowed and disced over and over so that there is hardly any grass left in the orchards (except in uncared for ranches). Around here, most of the fruit orchards are simply choking with grass and weeds, some of them towering above your head. The farmers here claim that the weeds and the grass retain the moisture in the soil and are thus beneficial to the orchards. For this reason, in comparison with the California fruit, there are more worms and bugs on the fruit trees and in the fruit. I believe that California fruit is far superior in taste and quality, although the Utahans have other ideas.

We built a large chicken coop and a pigpen to house the fifty chickens and eight pigs which we bought. The chickens, however, didn't live long since fried chicken came constantly to our minds whenever we saw them pecking around. Hence, the banquet which followed a few weeks later. The pigs survived longer since there were no butchers among us.

Two goats were purchased for five dollars apiece since we wanted some fresh goat milk every day. A few weeks later, a stray goat joined them. The family was increased last summer by the addition of two cute frisky babies, but since all of them escaped from the pigpen (they were kept together with the pigs) by jumping over the fence and destroyed some of our carrot crops, we finally got rid of the five goats for a total sum of five dollars. Some profit, huh?

It is true when you hear that Utah has only three snowless months. They are June, July, and August. I remember that we had to plant peas during the month of May while it was still snowing. We had the first snow of the season on September 9.

Our religious activities were not at all curtailed nor diminished. Reverend Edward White, minister of the Community Church in Park City, was kind enough to offer his services to us, and we held church meetings every Sunday morning. He was a Methodist preacher. We have in our group quite a few active religious Nisei from Monterey and Lompoc who have contributed immensely to the success of our religious activities. All of us didn't attend church, though, including yours truly. We had a standing agreement among us that all who wished to attend church may do so. Others were to work in the fields since we were working seven days a week then. All church goers were excused from work. Reverend White was with us till summer at which time he was transferred to Wyoming. Among the distinguished religious leaders who have honored us here at Keetley were Dr. Galen M. Fisher of Berkeley, Reverend Ernest Chapman of Salt Lake City, Reverend Arnold Katsuo Nakajima, formerly of San Francisco and Berkeley, and Reverend Ota of Salt Lake City. An old classmate of mine also visited us.

I hope that what little I know about the Mormon religion will interest you, Ophelia. Mormonism is like any other Christian religion. The children who have attended the Mormon Church at Heber City after Reverend White was transferred, were first taught the origin of this faith. It was founded by Joseph Smith, who is considered a prophet by the Mormons, many years ago in the state of Massachusetts. The story goes that one night Joseph Smith was given a stone tablet with the Words of God inscribed on it by an angel named Moroni who visited him. This stone tablet was similar to the Ten Commandments which was given to Moses. Moroni asked Joseph Smith to keep it for him until he returned for it. Joseph

Smith read it through and through and then translated it before Moroni came back for it some time later. His works, called the "Book of Mormon," is now held sacred by the Mormons equally with the Holy Bible. While preaching his beliefs, he was suspected of witchcraft by the townspeople. He was persecuted and later put to death.

Among the people at his trial was Brigham Young who sincerely believed in Joseph Smith's ideas. He reasoned that someone must carry on the works of Joseph Smith, and he vowed that he would be the person to do so. If he remained in Massachusetts, he would also be persecuted. Therefore, to escape such persecution, he organized a group of his followers to emigrate westward into the promised land where he wanted his group to settle down and live with freedom of worship. For months, they traveled westward in quest of suitable farming land. By the time they reached the vicinity of Salt Lake, they had encountered so many hardships that they couldn't go on any further. So they decided to settle here. The following year the colony started farming. A very large bumper crop resulted. Just before harvesting time, the entire countryside was plagued with swarms of locusts which started to destroy their crops. Unable to find suitable means of combating these pests, Brigham Young knelt down and prayed to the Lord for help and guidance. Then behold! A flock of seagulls came flying overhead and being hungry, they swooped down among the locusts and ate them, thereby saving the crops. Brigham Young's prayers had been answered! Today the seagulls are held sacred by the Mormons and a gold statue, the only kind in the world, is dedicated to the seagulls in the Temple Square in Salt Lake City.

A college dedicated to Brigham Young, Brigham Young University, is located in the city of Provo. Other colleges of major importance in Utah are the University of Utah in Salt Lake City and the Utah State Agricultural College in Logan.

In the beginning of May, my father was released from the internment camp at Missoula, Montana. A total of nine men whose wives and families were here in Keetley had been interned at the outbreak of the war. Subsequently four of them have been released and joined our colony here in Utah.

At this time, a group of thirty people left Keetley to start their farming project at Sandy, about 12 miles south of Salt Lake City. This still left approximately a hundred people in Keetley. Most of the young girls who have graduated from high school left for Salt Lake City to take domestic jobs where they were in great demand.

As we look back into the personnel of our group, we find a cross-section of California residents. We were from San Franciso, Oakland, Monterey, San Jose, and Lompoc. Later people from Point Reyes, Terminal Island, and Venice joined us. Ophelia, there were girls of all descriptions and shapes here--tall, short, plump, and skinny. But I suppose I have to admit that there are lots of nice looking damsels here especially from Monterey, San Jose and Lompoc (somebody's hinting that I should include San Francisco, too). I wonder sometimes what makes these girls so beautiful. Could it have been the climatic conditions or was it due to the Lompoc lettuce, San Jose prunes and the Monterey sardines?

A passage I recently read in your camp paper, "The Heart Mountain Sentinel", fittingly describes the types of legs the fairer sex possesses here at Keetley as "glamourous, beauteous." Hmmm . . . I wonder why all the girls here wear slacks! The girls have something to say about the boys too. They claim that knock-knees are very common among the Keetley boys. Just look at them in their basketball uniforms!

One of the girls here is so darn skinny, like a beanpole (and incidentally, very cute), that last spring the strong March wind almost blew her back to her hometown San Jose. We are always cautioned not to sneeze near her for fear that the draft may topple her.

In addition to Fred Wada's brothers, there are three other boys serving in our Armed Forces whose parents are here in Keetley. So far, all but one of them has been able to visit their families here. P.F.C. Bill Wada and Corporal Ben Wada came here on their furloughs together from Fort Benjamin Harrison, Indiana, and from Camp Grant, Illinois, in September. Sergeant Mas Honda of Lompoc visited his folks here in October from Camp Blanding, Florida. My older brother, Sergeant Katsumi Tsujimoto, arrived on the last day of December and spent New Year's Day with us. He was stationed at Fort Sam Houston, Texas. Corporal Tatsuji Yamada of San Jose was the only one not able to come home thus far. We are all awaiting his visit this year from Fort Sill, Oklahoma.

Two huge billboards bearing our advertisement and our slogan, "Food for Freedom," were built on the highway, and a large flagpole flying the Stars and Stripes has been erected. They have received many commendable reports from our white neighbors and passersby.

In May, a reporter and a photographer from the largest daily newspaper in the state of Utah, *The Salt Lake Tribune-Telegram*, came to visit our project. The morning issue is called the *Tribune* while the evening edition is called the *Telegram.* They took numerous pictures of us at work and at play. The June 6 issue of the *Salt Lake Telegram* carried an entire page of articles with several pictures of the progress made at

Keetley Farms. If I had your address, Ophelia, I would have been more than glad to send you a copy of it.

Concerning the pictures which appeared in that newspaper, we had a very humorous incident which proved to be embarrassing to a certain person. We sent a reprint of that edition to my brother in Fort Sam Houston, Texas, last summer. A few weeks later my sister received a letter from one of my brother's buddies in camp (none of us knew him) who introduced himself with a little bit of his personal background. He was a 1937 University of California graduate. At the conclusion of his letter, he stated that he happened to see the pictures appearing in the paper that we sent to our brother. He was particularly interested in one of the pictures that showed a group of six girls and ladies knitting for the American Red Cross. The paper naturally printed the names of the people appearing in the pictures, but they omitted whether they were Miss or Mrs. Of all the beautiful women in the picture, this poor soldier picked the married one (of course, he didn't know) and asked my sister to arrange it so that he could correspond with the specified girl. Somebody's face was sure red, deep in the heart of Texas, when he found out his error a few weeks later.

We have a very active girls' glee club which can boast of a number of classy nisei nightingales. They take certain pride in singing our official 'Keetley Valley" song which is very similar to and is set to the music of "Sleepy Valley". It has been arranged by Fred Wada and goes like this:

Keetley Valley

Everybody loves a fireside
Picture sitting by a fireside
In a cozy little home
You can call your own.
There's a place called Keetley, Utah
Let's go down to Keetley Valley
Angels picked this little spot
Where we chose to cast our lot.

Refrain:

Just a cozy farm
Sweet and heaven blessed
Like a bluebird's nest
In Keetley Valley.
Love is everywhere
Happiness is here
Love beyond compare
In Keetley Valley
All of my troubles
Cares of the day
Like silver bubbles
Drifting away
Snow around the door
Babies on the floor
Who could ask for more
Than Keetley Valley.

Most of us have been on a vegetable ranch for the first time in our lives, especially us city folks. During the time we weeded our carrot patch, I couldn't tell the difference between the carrot plants and the tiny sprouting weeds. Veteran farmers had to tell me which were the carrots and which were the weeds. They were both about the same size and color and looked very much alike. One of them was a little lighter, I can't remember which now. They were both growing uniformly in straight rows. To tell you the truth, they were as indistinguishable as a pair of Monterey sisters here in Keetley who are about the same size, both have dimples, look almost alike, and dress exactly alike. The only difference is that they respond to different names and one usually grins while the other usually pouts. They were only a fish dealer's daughters, but unlike what their father used to sell, were they fresh!

Summertime was our busiest season. By then, the vegetables have to be harvested. The home ranch was intrusted into the care of about ten men and all the womenfolk and children of the colony. I remained in Keetley throughout the year. Everyone young and old helped in the farm work. Ten year old kids to men who have seen seventy-five summers worked side by side. In fact, there is one grandmother past sixty who worked just as hard as any of us. She's a tiny lady weighing twenty pounds less than a sack of rice but who has more vigor than a young pup. She's only four feet five but alive like a beehive. Physically she resembles and sometimes is called the "Japanese Pansy Yokum". The latter smokes a corn cob pipe; the former rolls her own.

Practically all the men went to work at a sugarbeet ranch which we had contracted with at Spanish Fork, fifty miles south of Keetley.

They came home to help us on weekends. In addition to the two hundred and fifty acre ranch at Spanish Fork, we also had contracted with a seventy-five acre fruit orchard at Orem, about ten miles north of Spanish Fork. Six or seven of our men worked on this ranch raising apples, peaches, apricots, raspberries, tomatoes, potatoes, onions, etc.

Spanish Fork was by no means without humorous incidents. One of them happened one day when Fred Wada and a couple of men went to contact a large farm owner about farm labor. Our group received the jobs all right, but the big shot also asked Fred if he could send a young school-aged kid to care for his garden. Fred replied that since we were all pretty busy in Keetley, including kids fifteen years old, he couldn't spare any boys. Whereupon the boss took a good look at one of the men with Fred who was barely five feet tall and told Fred that even this little boy would do. Imagine the embarrassment of both parties concerned when it was explained that this "boy" was thirty-two years old, married, and the father of a four year old son! Since then, this fellow raised a fuzz under his nose.

Every day white farmers came to Keetley asking us to help them with their harvest. We were short-handed, but we helped a few of them. Young girls, some only eleven years old, went to work on other farms picking raspberries and strawberries. Kids ten years old and even younger helped to wash carrots and shell peas during the summer months.

An interesting and embarrassing incident occurred one day while we were busy washing and packing the carrots. While I was packing them in bushel baskets, I accidentally dropped one of those big, long yellowish-orange carrots, and I stooped to pick it up. You should have seen my embarrassment as well as that of the other party when by mistake, I grabbed the leg of one of the girls working with me. Somebody sure screamed! After all, they both looked so much alike in color and in shape! The only difference was that the carrot was raised in Keetley and the leg in Monterey.

We were sure busy then. We worked from six in the morning, and sometimes from five in the morning, till six at night. Many a time we worked till 8 p.m. and sometimes as late as 10:30 p.m. Once I worked till 12:30 a.m. That was the time we had to irrigate our lettuce patch under moonlit skies. Yes, we sure produced a lot of vegetables, but the markets of Salt Lake City were too small to handle all our vegetables. You must remember that the entire population of Utah is the size of San Francisco's population alone. The Safeway stores used lots of our crops. Some of our carrots were even shipped to Topaz Relocation Center. We gave quite a few of our fresh vegetables to our white neighbors who sure appreciated them. A basketful of our assorted fresh produce was also presented to Governor Maw last summer.

Our sagebrush-studded hills were not idle in the meantime. They were rented out to livestock owners. I believe that more than twenty thousand heads of sheep have grazed on our ranch. The largest single flock consisted of seven thousand five hundred head. There are also many cattle grazing in the pastures. Even in January of this year, a large herd of cattle was kept here in a snow-covered pasture. The cowpuncher naturally has to feed them twice a day by dropping a few sled-loads of hay all over the pasture. About a dozen milk cows are kept in the herd. They are milked daily, by the cowpuncher. This milk is sold to the "Hi-Land Dairy Co." of Murray, south of Salt Lake City. We buy the milk after it is pasteurized, cartoned, and delivered to our Keetley grocery store.

The pastures are criss-crossed with numerous small irrigating ditches, and last spring we had a tough time cleaning and digging them. Most of our water supply originates from natural springs, and since our vegetable crops require additional large amounts of water, we had to enlarge those springs. During the summer, with our water supply dwindling away, we had to clean the ditches in our pastures to decrease waste of water amid swarms of so-called "deer flies" which bite like mosquitoes. You can't shoo them off by swishing with your arms either; they're very stubborn (just like some of the Keetley nisei girls here). If you don't swat and kill each and every one of them, by night you will have a swollen face, neck, arms, and hands--and will be plenty itchy too. I remember that we were working half of the time; the other half of the time, we were busy swatting the pesky "deer flies".

Another pest that we all feared were the ticks, which were crawling all over our pastures. They are parasites preying on the sheep and they are always on the sagebrush. Practically all of us had ticks on our bodies at one time or another after we walked through the pastures. However, none of us suffered any illness from their bites.

Fred Wada

Since spring I have been the official mailman of our community and went after the mail a mile and a half to the Keetley post office right after lunch. Since the Postmaster of Keetley also worked in the mines, his post office hours were from 12:30 p.m. to 1:00 p.m. Incidentally, he had a very sweet, nice-looking daughter, (uhmmmmmmmm). She was only a Postmaster's daughter, but can she handle the males!

As the summer months gradually faded into autumn, the scenery around Keetley changed. The mountains took on a different hue. The leaves of the maple and the scrub oak trees changed to a deep red color and the entire mountainside was dotted with beautiful red patches. A sprinkling of bright yellow spots was intermixed among them due to the leaves of the ash trees. It was indeed a breathtaking sight.

Fall found us still busy with the harvest. We were able to can the last of our pea crop for home consumption. A cooperative cannery operated by the Mormon Church group in Heber City offered to can our peas at cost price (including empty cans and their supervision) of five cents per can. We have canned about fifteen hundred tins. Since the peas that were to be canned had to be very freshly shelled, I remember that we all had to get up at four o'clock in the morning for two days to shell them.

On the last day of August, I was suddenly affected by an acute case of streptococcus infection of blood poisoning in my right foot. It was probably caused by an insect bite. After six incisions and almost five months of recuperation, I finally completely recovered at the end of January of this year. It was sure tiresome and boring doing nothing every day while recuperating. I had to wile away the time by doing jigsaw puzzles, crossword puzzles, writing letters, and even helped a certain party in knitting her socks! I knitted only sixteen stitches, but after all, sixteen stitches are sixteen stitches!

In September, the first of the Tanforan Assembly Center residents came to Topaz Relocation Center, Utah, which made all of us very glad since most of our San Francisco and Bay Region friends, including one of my brothers, were at Tanforan. We visited Topaz on numerous occasions. I went there twice, once on an overnight trip. I have enjoyed seeing and talking with my many friends and have seen the entire camp. I really do know now how life must be like at Heart Mountain Relocation Center, Ophelia. Topaz Relocation Center is about one hundred and fifty five miles southwest of Keetley. Due to the thirty-five miles per hour war speed limit, however, the trip requires about four to five hours. The scenery en route to Topaz is very dull-

-nothing but sagebrush and desert, but it is worth the trip to meet our uncountable number of friends. I wish that we could make the trip to Heart Mountain, but with the gas rationing in effect, I know that it is impossible. Some friends of ours now residing in Provo, which is near Spanish Fork, were able to motor up the five hundred mile trip to your camp last October.

During the fall and winter, our personnel here has changed quite a bit. In early October, three men joined us from Granada Relocation Center, Colorado, and helped us in our farm work. In mid-November they went to settle on a ranch at Spanish Fork where the three men are planning to farm this spring with their families who will be released from Granada this year. At the end of October, my younger brother was released from the Topaz Relocation Center and joined us with an Oakland fellow. In November, six more people came here from Idaho. They were working in the sugarbeet fields there on furlough from the Manzanar Relocation Center, California.

Last year two babies were born here in Keetley, a boy and a girl. Their parents were from Lompoc and Oakland. In December the entire population from Lompoc with the exception of one family left Keetley for Spanish Fork to begin their own farming project. There were about twenty-five people in this group.

Due to the present situation, our social activities are very much limited. In May, a combination farewell party for the group that left Keetley for Sandy and a welcome party for my father who returned from Montana was held. This was the first time that all of us ever dined together. Practically all of us were strangers before we came to Keetley, but by now we were beginning to become better acquainted. Besides the wiener bake sponsored by the American Keetley boys, we had a combination steak barbecue, wiener roast, and watermelon bust by a small creek on our ranch. This was on the Fourth of July. Before this, we had a picnic at Luke's Hot Pot, a nearby Hot Springs Resort, about fifteen miles from Keetley. We spent the day swimming, eating, and playing games. On Labor Day, we had another steak barbecue in honor of Fred's two brothers who were here on their furloughs from the Army camps.

Practically every evening, games of some sort are going on here. They may be card games, Mah Jong, or something like that. All night poker sessions are very common. It seems that every once in awhile, somebody's old man is thrown out on his ear by the person who wears the pants in the family when he returns in the wee hours of the morning. We have seen several home movies here. Mr. Fisher took a movie picture in color of us at work and at play last summer during the harvest season which turned out exceptionally well. A few of the unposed candid shots were the source of much laughter among us when we reviewed the films.

We once went on a so-called "snipe hunt". One of the poor kibei suckers was the goat. We took him one moonlit evening deep into our sagebrushed pasture. We gave him a burlap potato sack and told him to hold it over one of the numerous holes dug by the prairie dogs. Naturally we told him that it was a "snipe-hole" and that they were a cinch to come out on moonlit nights. We even lit a match for him to "attract the snipe". Then we told him that the rest of us would go further up in the hills and stamp on the ground in order to chase the poor critter out of the hole. The kid fell for it, hook, line, and sinker. In the meantime, the rest of us circled back to our ranch and went to bed. Was he sore the next morning? And how! He stayed there by the hole for two hours holding the sack. I bet he sure looked silly. We had to treat him to cokes and cookies to put him in the right humor.

Remember Dr. Henry Takahashi, who used to have his optometrist shop next to my drugstore, the Misawa Pharmacy, in San Francisco? He visited us at Keetley in early November. He received a ride here with the Miyoshi sisters of Murray from Salt Lake City. These girls evacuated to Murray from Sacramento, California at about the same time we came to Utah last spring. Henry was in

Salt Lake City on a week's furlough from the Topaz Relocation Center. Director Charles F. Ernst of Topaz was also a visitor at Keetley in November.

Later in the month, two girls came here for a few weeks' stay from Topaz. One was from Oakland and the other was from San Francisco. They enjoyed themselves, indulging in the winter sports here and shopping in Salt Lake City and Heber City.

Farm work was completed here at the end of October, and the aim and the goal of our Keetley Farms have been successfully attained. We have produced more than our share of the "Food for Freedom". All the workers returned to Keetley from Spanish Fork and Orem. Since then the members of the colony have been doing odd jobs here and there. Some went to Spanish Fork again to top sugarbeets. Some went to Provo to prune fruit trees. Others went to Park City for mining jobs. Still others went to Salt Lake City (including my brothers) to work in metal salvage jobs. The latter two are national defense jobs, so enough gasoline for commuting purposes were allowed them on "B" and "C" gas ration cards. I received a "B" gas ration card to see my doctor at Heber City twice a week for my foot treatment.

The weather got colder and colder as the days passed by. The snow-covered ground was freezing fast. Melted snow solidified into large areas of ice. We all had to walk carefully as slips and spills became a common sight in Keetley Valley. At one time an aged man from San Jose slipped on the ice and received a nasty cut on his head which required medical attention. At another time a grandpappy also hailing from the same locality took a spill on the ice. However, his case was quite different. One day as he was walking along the ice-covered road carrying his tiny granddaughter, a large dog belonging to one of our white neighbors, which takes delight in retrieving objects thrown by anyone, approached him with a big chunk of rock. He wagged his tail and looked beseechingly at the grandpappy to throw him the rock. Since his hands were occupied, he tried to kick the rock away so that the dog could run and retrieve it. But I suppose he miscalculated the distance of the rock for he took a mighty kick, missed the rock completely, and slipped, landing flat on his back. He was knocked senseless for a minute or two. The baby, on the other hand, was flung up but fortunately landed smack on her grandpappy's belly--and stayed there cooing. If one is not used to walking in the snow and ice, it is a safe bet that the party will take a flop. When a couple of visitors came here from Topaz Relocation Center a few months ago, one of them took a very pretty flop on her seat which left a very clear-cut imprint on the snow. Perhaps she had meant to leave a memento of herself in Keetley Valley. As the saying goes, "the bigger they are, the harder they fall."

Keetley can justly be called a sportsman's winter paradise. Since November, snow has piled up here. At this time, all the tiny tots are enjoying themselves sledding down the snow-covered slopes. They were naturally joined in their fun by the older folks. In December, a five foot toboggan was added to our winter sports equipment, and the older kids had much fun on it going down the long, steep hills, although daily casualties were relatively heavy.

In one instance, three girls went right through a barbed wire fence (the space between the wires was about seven inches) and came out on the other side of the fence with numerous cuts on their hands, faces, arms, and legs. Nope, the girls weren't that skinny; the wires of the fence were pretty loose, thank heavens! One of the girls didn't go through, though; she just hit the fence post--and stayed there, the hefty thing! Outside of minor scratches, torn slacks, torn boots, torn jackets, torn mittens, etc., the girls weren't so badly hurt. The girls had their eyes closed because of the snow which flew in their faces and therefore didn't know that they were approaching the fence. Everything happened so suddenly. When the gal who didn't go through the fence opened her eyes, the first thing she saw was a piece of somebody's slacks dangling on the barbed wires in front of her eyes. The boys had their share of the injuries too. One kid couldn't get up for quite awhile after a very bad spill. He hit his tail-bone pretty hard; one kid sprained his thumb; a kid broke his eyeglasses and received cuts on his face. Practically everyone who has ridden on the toboggan bears scars or scratches of one sort or another as souvenirs.

After Christmas Day, all the kids started buying ice skates since we have a very large frozen pond near our place. The area of this natural ice skating rink is more than one square city block. Most of us were beginners, with a few exceptions, but the kids sure learned fast. Spills are getting less and less frequent day after day. It won't be long before we all become experts. Due to my present foot condition, I'm about the only one who has never worn a pair of ice skates.

Watching my sister learning how to skate was very interesting. The skates insisted on moving ahead, but the part of her anatomy that passes through the doorway last (not the heels, either) had other ideas, resulting in a one point landing plus a wet pair of slacks. In another instance, a San Jose beauty was being taught by her big brother how to skate on her brand new pair of skates. This was her first experience on the ice. Having been told to grab her brother's outstretched hands, she complied willingly, but somehow she was groping around for the hands which weren't there. Results? Well, down she went as the Law of Gravity took effect. Yup, she quit ice skating for a few weeks. Of course, again, as the saying goes, "the taller they are, the more distance they have to fall."

Most of the people here are being economical on the wear and tear on their ice skates, especially one of the two lovely sisters hailing from the San Jose Valley. She spends considerable time gliding on her seat instead of on the skates--intentionally or not, I do not know.

A few of the kids also bought some skis and practiced daily. Skiing, one of the newer winter sports among us, made an immense hit with everyone here. Most of us had a few tries at them--some of us with real success. I suppose the main trouble with the beginners in skiing is that the skis insist on separating, one wishing to go one way and the mate the other way.

We have entered a basketball team in the Salt Lake City J.A.C.L. league made up of nisei teams in and near Salt Lake City. So far, in the first half, we are not faring so well, but the second half may find the Keetley team bringing home the bacon--if it isn't rationed by then.

In mid-November, the operator of the Keetley grocery store, the O'Tooles, moved to Ogden, where Mr. O'Toole received a war defense industry job, and an Italian family moved in and took over the grocery store. The newcomers, the Bert Cattelans, were formerly store operators at Oakley, ten miles northeast of Keetley. They are well-liked by all of us and give us excellent service, just like their predecessors. Since Bert was an experienced butcher (he brought along his two pigs), he helped us butcher and dress one of our eight pigs. The pork was divided and enjoyed by all of us here. Some of the families had roast pork dinners on Thanksgiving Day. Last month

Bert killed one of the pigs, and I helped him make some pork sausage out of it which was very, very tasty; in fact it was the best pork sausage we ever ate.

The butchering of the pigs reminds me of an unusual sight I encountered when the cowpuncher taking care of a herd of cattle in our ranch had to shoot one of his mares which was kicked in the leg by another horse and consequently suffered a broken leg. I saw the bone sticking out of her broken skin. After shooting her, the cowpuncher took out a sharp knife and skinned the dead horse. I suppose the hide weighed more than a hundred pounds. Since this mare had been pregnant, an unborn colt which may have been in her womb for six months or so, was found. It was a perfectly formed, cute colt and the white spots characteristic of his mother clearly appeared on his nose. He probably weighed about forty pounds. The hide was sold to a skin dealer while the carcass was sold to a mink farm to feed the minks. Both were sold for a sum of five dollars a piece.

Presently no one is working here so all the older kids are indulging daily in the winter sports. The old timers are taking it easy, including yours truly. Our community always has a noisy atmosphere due to the dozen or so tiny tykes ranging from two years old to five years old who are competing daily in bawling (not bowling) marathons. In this sport, my younger nephew tops them all, although the competition is very keen. However, the hustle and the bustle of Keetley, is considerably increased after the school kids come home.

The children are attending either the North Elementary School, the Central Elementary School, or the Wasatch High School, all at Heber City. The high school is a combination of junior and senior high schools. The kids are commuting daily, and even on some Saturdays, by one of the county school buses which is kept in a garage behind the grocery store here at Keetley. The bus driver resides here in our neighborhood.

The kids are getting along very nicely at school.

Several girls received all "A's" on their report cards. They're only farmers' daughters, but they sure know their onions! One of the girls was elected captain of her grammar school's girls' baseball team by her teammates. Last year one of our nisei boys ran for the office of president of his eighth grade class at Wasatch High School and lost by a very close margin, coming in second. Such instances bring out the fact that here in Wasatch County the nisei kids get along and associate a lot with their white classmates.

Many of our girls are taking snapshots of themselves taken in California to school and are exchanging them with those of their new white classmates. Whenever we go to Heber City for shopping, the passersby, especially kids we never saw before, stop and say "Hello" to us. Last year when a Heber City druggist displayed in his store windows photographs of Heber City boys and men in the Armed Forces. He cordially offered to display pictures of our five boys serving in the U.S. Army from Keetley, which was indeed a very friendly gesture on his part.

On the other hand, the group that left Keetley for Sandy in the spring of last year is riding on a horse of a different color. They have among them an excellent basketball player who had earned the first string guard berth on the high school varsity basketball team there. However, he was asked to leave the team after a few games due to public sentiments, although the coach had no personal feelings against this nisei player. I'm sure that no such incidents will ever happen here at Wasatch High School.

New Year's Day was spent in an appropriate manner. All the families pooled their "shogatsu no gochiso," and we had a very large banquet proceeded by bingo and other games, at which time numerous prizes were awarded. Yours truly came home with more merchandise then he could carry alone. The banquet was complete with all the food we used to have back home in San Francisco on New Year's Day. Speeches, songs, and other forms of entertainment were added to the program. We had more food than we could eat. In fact, one tiny Monterey Miss misjudged her digestive capacity and ate so much that day that she was disabled the following morning with a bad case of tummyache.

A few of the families had their pictures taken early in January. All of them came out swell. Enclosed you will find some very interesting pictures of some of us enjoying the snow as well as a few snapshots of Keetley Valley in wintertime. In one of the family pictures which I happened to see, the youngest boy in the family, a seventeen year old punk, was so tall that he stuck out like a sore thumb, another Monterey product.

The Tsujimoto Farmhouse in Keetley

Ophelia, I must mention the Great Salt Lake to you before I forget. Next to the Dead Sea in Palestine, the Great Salt Lake, west of Salt Lake City, is the saltiest body of water in the world. In prehistoric times, a great inland body of water, which has been designated as Lake Bonneville, covered an area in the Great Basin about ten times as large as the present Great Salt Lake. The present lake is about seventy-five miles long and thirty-five miles wide. By evaporation, the water became saltier and saltier, until it has reached a density of approximately 25%. A human body floats in it as light as a cork. There is no more refreshing bathing in the world than in the Great Salt Lake.

Here in Keetley, we have had unusually cold weather. In mid-January the mercury dropped to minus twenty degrees which is fifty-two degrees below freezing point. No wonder I had to wake up in the middle of the night, put on my scarf, and wear my knitted snowcap so that my ears wouldn't slough off. Even though a fire was blazing away in the stove in the adjoining room , the temperature in our bedroom was ten degrees, or twenty -two degrees below freezing point. Our water systems were all frozen, and the following morning practically every pipe burst. We sure realized the conveniences of the good ole two-by-four greenhouses then. Yup, they're serviceable twelve months a year, especially out here.

All play and no work makes Jack a dull boy, so we shovel the snow and clear the paths once in awhile. Dark goggles are necessary since we're liable to get snow blinded if we stay out in the snow too long. This reminds me of an Oakland lassie here in Keetley who is perpetually squinting or winking her eyes. Of course, this could be the result of her habit of making eyes at the boys around here!

As I look out of the window now, I can see the entire neighborhood and the distant mountains completely enveloped by a white blanket of snow. I can just sit and visualize what is in store for us here in Keetley this year. During the past year, lots of water has floated under our bridge, and we are all looking forward to the arrival of spring so that we can again do our utmost to raise more "Food for Freedom".

Well, Ophelia, I guess I covered just about everything there is to tell you about us here at Keetley Valley so I better call it "30" now. Here's hoping that you will be able to write to me in your spare time . . .

Very sincerely yours,

Mas

AMERICAN COUNCIL
INSTITUTE OF PACIFIC RELATIONS
260 CALIFORNIA STREET SAN FRANCISCO

Feb. 15/43

Dear Mr. Fujimoto—

What a vivid and engaging chronicle you have written! It is good to see that your sense of humor and your charity have not been dimmed by all the tough things you all have been through.

I showed your chronicle to Dr. Thomas at U.C., who is directing a scientific study of the entire evacuation and she was eager to read it, so I sent it to her. Probably she will wish to copy portions of it. I told her you would, of course, be glad to have it used.

What sobering yet stimulating thoughts Lincoln's birthday always arouses. May our people live up far better to his noble ideals!

Sincerely yours, Galen M. Fisher.

GALEN M. FISHER
11 EL SUENO
ORINDA, CALIFORNIA

Feb. 11, 1943

Dear Mr. Tsuyemoto—

I shall look forward eagerly to using your chronicle. Thank you for taking the trouble to type it all out for me.

What a marvelous year you have had — hard at elections and a substantial contribution to the nation's war effort!

Sincerely yours
Galen M. Fisher

Name	Former address	Present address
1. Toyoko Fujimoto	San Francisco	Keetley, Utah
2. Noboru Dakata	Monterey	Keetley, Utah
3. [illegible] Yamada	Oakland	Keetley, Utah
4. William Takagawa	Monterey	Keetley, Utah
5. Koji Kita	Venice	Keetley, Utah
6. Mitsuko Takigawa	Monterey	Keetley, Utah
7. Satsuki Takigawa	Monterey	Keetley, Utah
8. Kazuko Okamoto	San Jose	Keetley, Utah Keetley, Utah
9. Toshiko Yamada	San Jose	Keetley, Utah
10. May Yamada		
11. Kay K. Takenaka	San Jose Suisun	Keetley, Utah
12. Sam Kitabayashi	Suisun	Heart Mt., Wyo.
13. Mary Jio	San Jose	Heart Mt., Wyoming
14. Joe K. Jio	San Jose, Calif.	Heart Mt., Wyoming
15. Benson Fujioka	Los Angeles, Calif.	Heart Mt., Wyo.
16. Etsuko Nakano	San Francisco	Heart Mt., Wyoming
17. Arline Takata	San Francisco	Heart Mountain, Wyoming
18. Michi Tamaru	San Francisco	Heart Mountain
19. Nancy Yonemura	Los Angeles	Heart Mountain
20. Yuriko Tanaka	Hollywood	Heart Mt.
21. Agnes Inouye	San Francisco	Heart Mountain
22. Frank Kumamoto	Los Angeles	Heart Mt. Wyo
23. Albert S. Tanouye	Los Angeles	Heart Mt., Wyo
24. John Y. Furuta	[illegible]	Heart Mt. Wyo
25. Kiyoko Shimane	San Jose	Heart Mt. Wyo.

	Name	Former address	Present address
26.	Miori Shimine	San Jose	Heart Mt., Wy.
27.	Alyce Shimine	San Jose	Heart Mt., Wy.
28.	Sumi Kurasaki	San Jose	Heart Mt, Wyo.
29.	S. Ohno	Riverside	Heart Mt, Wyo.
30.	Masa Ohno	Riverside	Heart Mt., Wyoming
31.	Miyo Sakaji	Los Angeles	Heart Mt, Wyo.
32.	Frank Ito	Fresno	Heart Mt.
33.	Arthur T. Morimoto	Sacramento, Calif	Newell, Calif (Tule Lake)
34.	Koro Yatsu	Sacramento	Newell, Calif.
35.	Katherine Ishida	Sacramento, Calif.	Tule Lake, Newell, Calif
36.	Kazuo Kimura	Sacramento, Calif	Tulelake Calif.
37.	Pfc. Katsumi Fujimoto	San Francisco	Camp Shelby, Miss.
38.	George K. Mukai	Folsom Calif	Poston Unit II. Ari
39.	Ray Ryoichi Mori	Sacramento,	Poston, Arizona. II
40.	Yoneko Florence Yamauchi	Sacramento	Poston, Arizona II
41.	Michiko Helen Yamasaki	Sacramento, California	Poston, Arizona Camp II
42.	May Y. Ogawa	Sacramento, California	Poston, Arizona #2.
43.	Ruby Kaneno	Folsom, California	Poston Arizona
44.	Daisy Nakahara	Loomis Calif.	Poston. Arizona #2
45.	Shizuye Matsuda	Sacramento, Calif.	Poston Arizona #2
46.	Sue Kobayashi	Sacramento, Calif.	Poston, Arizona II
47.	Betty [illegible]	Sacramento Calif.	Poston Arizona [illegible]
48.	Mary Nitta	Natomas, California	Poston Arizona #2
49.	Alice Hatakeda	Pismo Beach, Calif	Poston, Arizona #2
50.	Kei Harada	Sacramento, Calif.	Poston, Ari[illegible]

	Name	Former Address	Present Address
51.	[illegible]	Sacramento, Calif.	Poston Arizona
52.	Akiro [illegible]	Sacramento Calif.	Poston Ariz. #2
53.	James K. Hirota	Sacramento Calif	Poston, Ariz #2
54.	Frank S. Deguchi	Sacramento, Calif.	Poston, Ariz #2
55.	Tom I. Kawamura	Sac'to Calif.	Poston, Ariz. #2
56.	Kenji Harada	alias "Rocky"	Poston, Ariz.
57.	Edward K. Inouye	Sac'to, Calif.	Poston – Ariz
58.	Masatomo Kawahara	Sacto Calif.	Poston Ariz.
59.	Amy Kaneno	Folsom Calif	Poston Ariz #
60.	Chiyo Kaneno	Folsom Calif	Poston, Ariz
61.	Ichiro Nakayama	Sacto Calif.	Poston Ariz
62.	[illegible]	Sacto Calif.	Poston Ariz
63.	Harry Nabeshima	Sacto, Calif	Poston Ariz
64.	George [illegible]	Sacto, Calif	Poston Ari
65.			Poston, Ariz
66.	Ace Nakamura	Watsonville	
67.	Mary Kuwabara	Sacramento	Poston Arizo
68.	Sid Shiratsuki	Salinas	Poston Arizona
69.	Tayeko Hironaka	Sacramento	Poston Arizona
70.	Miyako Hironaka	Sacramento	Poston, Arizona
71.	[illegible]	Sacramento	Poston Ariz / Poston, Arizona
72.	[illegible] Hironaka	Sacramento	Poston, Ariz
73.	Yuriko Hironaka	Sacramento	Poston, Ariz
74.	Harry [illegible]	Sacramento	Poston Ariz
75.	Mitsuye [illegible]	Sacramento	Poston Ariz

	Name	Former Address	Present Address
6.	Albert Y. Ueda [illegible]		
7.	Chiyeko Teramoto	Woodland	Poston II, Arizona
8.	May Sunakara	Sacramento	Poston, Arizona
9.	Mas J. Sunakara	Sacramento	Poston, Arizona
.	[illegible]	[illegible]	229-11-A [illegible]
1.	Yoshiko Terakawa	Salinas	Poston, Arizona
.	Masayuki Matsumune	Salinas	Poston, Arizona
.	May Ikeda	Salinas	Poston, Arizona
4.	[illegible]		[illegible]
5.	[illegible] Terakawa	Salinas	Poston, Arizona
.	Mary Cowr[illegible]	Dana Point	" , Arizona
.	Makiko Yamamoto	Watsonville, Calif.	Poston, Arizona
.	Michiko Takeuchi	Sacramento	Poston, Arizona - #2
9.	[illegible]	Santa Clara Cal.	[illegible]
.	[illegible] Takeuchi	Sacramento	Poston
1.	[illegible] Maruyama	Oakland, Calif.	Topaz, Utah
.	Chiyoko Kita	Lawndale, Calif.	Spanish Fork, Ut.
.	Tom Kita	Hawthorne	Spanish Fork
.	[illegible]	Monterey Calif.	Salt Lake City, Utah
5.			
.			
.			
8.			
.			
.			

Name	Former address	Present address
1. Hiroko Tsujimoto	San Francisco	Keetley, Utah.
2. [illegible] Takagawa	N. Monterey	Keetley, Utah
3. Fred I. Ota	Oakland Cal	Keetley Utah
4. Tom T. Maruyama	Oakland Calif.	Keetley, Utah
5. Masako Nishida	Oakland, Calif.	Topaz, Utah
6. [illegible]	Oakland, Calif.	Topaz, Utah
7. [illegible] Hayashi	Oakland Calif.	Topaz, Utah
8. Hiro Sato	Oakland, Calif.	Topaz, Utah
9. Shigeo Oka	Centerville, Calif	Topaz, Utah
10. Masao Tomotoshi	Mt Eden, Calif	Topaz Utah
11. Hisako Tomotoshi	Mt. Eden, Calif.	Topaz, Utah
12. Kay Tomatoshi	Mt. Eden, Calif.	Topaz, Utah
13.		
14. Yuki Minamoto	Oakland, Calif.	Topaz, Utah
15. Miyuki Maruyama	Oakland, California	Topaz, Utah.
16. Kaz Inouye	Oakland Calif.	Topaz, Utah
17. [illegible]	Los Angeles, Calif.	Topaz, Utah
18. Mary Fumi Maruyama	Oakland, Calif.	Topaz, Utah
19. Mitsuno Maruyama	Oakland, California	Topaz, Utah
20. Fred W. Tsujimoto	San Francisco, Calif.	Keetley, Utah.
21. Masami Maruyama	Oakland Calif	Topaz
22. N. Robert Yamada	Alameda Calif	Topaz, Utah
23. George Shinoda	Oakland, California	Topaz Utah
24. Iso Minamoto	Oakland, Calif.	Topaz, Utah
25. Helen Amai	San Francisco, Cal.	Topaz, Utah

Name	Former Address	Present Address
[illegible]	San Francisco, Calif.	Topaz, Utah
Chiyo [illegible]	San Francisco, Calif.	Topaz, Utah
S/SGT. BILL KAWAI	SAN FRANCISCO, CALIFORNIA	CAMP HALE, COLO.
Tokuji Hedani	San Francisco	Topaz
Bill Fujita	San Francisco	Topaz
Nobuo Renge		
George Arita	Fowler California / Sacramento, California	Denson, Arkansas / Jerome, Arkansas
Haruko Arita	Sacramento, California	Denson, Arkansas
Sylvia Arita	[illegible], Calif.	Jerome Relocation Center
Tamotsu Arase	Fresno, California	Denson, Arkansas
[illegible] Kunishige	Fresno California	Denson Arkansas
Mrs. Kearney Kunishige	Fresno, California	Denson, Arkansas
Toshiko [illegible]	Hanford Calif.	Denson, Ark.
Pfc. Jerry Sakohira	Fowler Calif.	Camp Robinson Ark.
Howard [illegible]	Fresno Calif.	Jerome W.R.A.
HATSUMI WADA	HANFORD, CALIFORNIA	DENSON, ARKANSAS
MAY ASAKI	HANFORD, CALIFORNIA	DENSON, ARKANSAS.
Fred Mizota	Alviso, California	Heart Mt. Wyo.
Martha S. [illegible]	San Francisco	Heart Mt. Wyo.
Asaye Mizota	Alviso, California	Heart Mt., Wyo.
Helen Mizota	Alviso California	Heart Mt Wyo.
Haruko Hirata	Santa Clara Calif.	Heart Mt. Wyo.
[illegible]	Monterey, California	Salt Lake City, Utah
Evelyn Yamanda	Monterey, California	Minneapolis, Minnesota

[illegible]	[illegible]	[illegible]
Pat O'Toole	Keetley, Utah	Ogden, Utah
Tello Nagatoshi	San Francisco	Chicago, Ill
Mary Yamanaka	Chicago, Ill.	Chicago, Ill
[illegible]	[illegible]	[illegible]
Julia Yamazaki	Chicago, Illinois	Chicago, Illinois
Pvt. Fumitsu Matsumoto	[illegible], Hawaii	Camp Savage, Minn
Pvt. Michi Kikudome	HAKALAU, Hawaii	Camp Savage, Minn.
Francis Ozoe	Chicago, Ill.	Chicago, Ill.
Pvt. Ernest H. Kimura	Honolulu, Hawaii	Camp Savage
Mary Rodgers	chicago, 10, Ill.	Chicago, Ill.
Emily A. Medal	Chicago, Ill.	Y.W.C.A. Aurora, Ill.
Mary [illegible]	Hawthorne, Calif.	Spanish Fork, Utah
Misa Kobata	Winters, California	Carmel, Cal.
Ophelia	San Francisco, Calif.	Heart Mt. Wyo
May Tanjimoto Kitagawa	March 27, 1968	New Orleans, La.
[illegible] Kitagawa	March 27, 1968	New Orleans, La.
[illegible]	3/[illegible]	[illegible]
Tatsuo S. Tanaka	1/27/88	Oakland, Calif

Name	Present Address	Former Address
Sgt. Bill Hada	Camp Savage, Minn.	Oakland, Calif.
Rose Kita	Gardena, California	Spanish Fork, Ut.

Made in the USA
San Bernardino, CA
01 June 2017